ERNESTO ZIERER

The Theory of Graphs in Linguistics

MOUTON

THE THEORY OF GRAPHS IN LINGUISTICS

JANUA LINGUARUM

STUDIA MEMORIAE
NICOLAI VAN WIJK DEDICATA

edenda curat

C. H. VAN SCHOONEVELD
INDIANA UNIVERSITY

SERIES MINOR
94

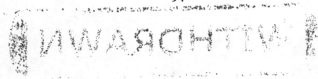

1970
MOUTON
THE HAGUE · PARIS

THE
THEORY OF GRAPHS
IN LINGUISTICS

by

ERNESTO ZIERER

NATIONAL UNIVERSITY OF TRUJILLO, PERU

1970
MOUTON
THE HAGUE · PARIS

Original title:
La teoria de los graficos en la linguistica

Translated from Spanish by Bernard Davis

LIBRARY OF CONGRESS CATALOG CARD NUMBER: 71-129294

Printed in The Netherlands by Mouton & Co., Printers, The Hague.

INTRODUCTION

Within the process of mathematisation which is occurring in certain sectors of linguistics, the THEORY OF GRAPHS is steadily becoming more important.

Granted that language is an essentially structural phenomenon, the Theory of Graphs turns out to be an adequate method for representing the properties of linguistic structures, facilitating the comprehension of structural relations in linguistics.

This publication is based on a seminar carried out in 1967 by members of the Department of Languages and Linguistics of the National University of Trujillo with the participation of Professor Alejandro Ortiz of the Faculty of Physical and Mathematical Sciences, whose valuable collaboration has contributed to the success of the seminar.

It is intended that this work should be merely an introduction, an essay, to present the reader with a new instrument for use in his linguistic studies.

An attempt has been made to accompany each new concept with one or several examples taken from linguistics, so that the reader may realise, step by step, which are the possibilities of application of the Theory of Graphs in linguistics.

TABLE OF CONTENTS

APPLICATION OF THE THEORY
OF GRAPHS IN LINGUISTICS

A. BASIC CONCEPTS

1. *Definition of graph:* A GRAPH is a figure which consists of points, also called VERTICES or NODES, and, generally, of lines, called SIDES or EDGES, which connect some or all of the points among them.

In the Theory of Graphs the term 'graph' has a different meaning from the one it has in analytical geometry, in the study of functions or in statistics. In the Theory of Graphs the graph serves to represent the organisation of some STRUCTURAL PHENOMENA thus making possible the discovery of analogous structures in the various branches of science. The expression of structural relations by graphs means a considerable SAVING IN THOUGHT PROCESSES.

Example 1: In Spanish the combination of the phonemes /a/ and /t/ can be represented by the following graph:

2. *Complete graph:* This is a graph in which every pair of different points is connected by a side.

Example 2: In Spanish the following combinations of phonemes are found:

/at/ : *at*leta	/ta/ : *ta*rde	/ar/ : *ta*rde
/ra/ : *ra*ta	/tr/ : *tr*ata	/rt/ : har*t*o

In Spanish no condition exists which imposes a restriction on the combination of the three phonemes /a/, /r/ and /t/.

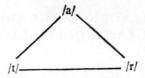

3. *Directed graph:* A graph in which a direction has been assigned to each edge is called a DIRECTED graph.

Example 3: The phonological system of Spanish does not admit the combination /sr/ (except in proper nouns like *Israel*) but it does admit /rs/: *arsénico, arsenal*

$$/r/ \longrightarrow /s/$$

4. *Empty graph:* A graph which has NO edges.

Example 4: The combination of the letters /s/ and /h/ is not admitted in Spanish.

o   o

/s/   /h/

5. *Mixed graph:* A graph in which some edges are directed and others are not.

Example 5: The following graph shows the admissible combinations of the phonemes /r/, /o/ and /s/ in Spanish:

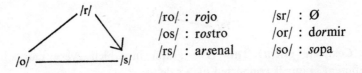

/ro/ : *rojo*	/sr/ : Ø
/os/ : *rostro*	/or/ : *dormir*
/rs/ : *arsenal*	/so/ : *sopa*

6. *Incomplete graph:* A graph which does not conform to the definition given above for the complete graph.

Example 6: In Spanish the phoneme /s'/ in the initial position cannot be combined with another consonantal phoneme. The graph which represents the combinations of /s'/, /e/, /a/, /t/ is incomplete:

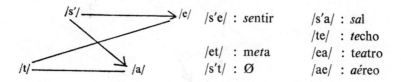

/s'e/ : *sentir*	/s'a/ : *sal*
	/te/ : *techo*
/et/ : *meta*	/ea/ : *teatro*
/s't/ : Ø	/ae/ : *aéreo*

7. *Complement of a graph:* A graph formed by all the edges (and points) which may be necessary to complete an incomplete graph.

Example 7: In the graph corresponding to Ex. 6, in which the condition that the phoneme /s'/ should be in the initial position is imposed, the complement is an empty graph. But if we eliminate this restriction, we can draw a directed side from /s/ to /t/ since the combination /st/ as in *hasta* exists.

8. *Arc:* A directed side on a graph.

Example 8: In a form analogous to the one which occurs in the flow of speech, the Spanish word *alto* can be considered as the result of a generative process, producing the corresponding sequence of the phonemes /a/, /l/, /t/, /o/:

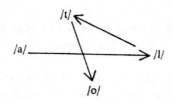

9. *Path:* The route of a graph which, although it may pass through the same points several times, never follows a side more than once.

Example 9: The representation of the Spanish word *altar* in the form analogous to Example 8:

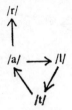

10. *Cyclic path:* A path which returns to its point of departure is a cyclic path.

Example 10: The generation of the sentence *El compra papas y ella vende naranjas* in the flow of speech can be represented by means of a graph with four arcs. Each arc represents a phase in the generative process, and the points represent the results up to this moment. In the first cycle of the path the first element of each pair corresponding to each arc is selected. The second cycle ends at the point of departure, generating the sign /./, which indicates the end of the sentence.

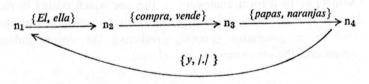

11. *Loop:* A graph formed by only one edge which begins and ends at only one point is called a loop.

12. *Multiple edges:* They are sides which in the form of loops or cyclic paths follow each other in succession more than once.

Example 11: In the following graph the edges represent certain 'word classes' according to the classification by Fries for the

English language.[1] The construction symbolised by means of the graph permits the generation of more than 10^{21} grammatical expressions. In the graph the class B_3 forms a loop. There are cyclic paths on the edges B_6-B_7 and B_9-B_{10}, as there is also one which departs from the point of origin P_0, passes through the point of articulation P_a, reaches the boundary P_m and returns to the point P_0 through the side B_{11}. The point of articulation P_a divides the syntactic construction into two members, within which occur the nodes from P_1 to P_5. The sides T_1 and T_2 are empty sides and only serve to prevent the sides B_6 and B_{10}, and B_9 and B_7 from following each other in a directly consecutive way.

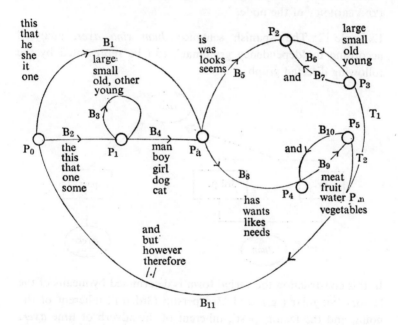

The syntactic construction represented by means of this graph can be symbolised in the following formula, in which the symbol $\neq$ indicates separation, parentheses indicate repetition of loops (or

[1] Example taken from: W. Meyer-Eppler, *Grundlagen und Anwendungen der Informationstheorie* (Berlin-Göttingen-Heidelberg, 1959), p. 343.

cyclic edges), and the symbol $| : \quad : |$, indicates repetition of a subconstruction (sequence of edges):

$$\left| \; : \; \begin{matrix} \#B_1 \\[1em] \#B_2(B_3)B_4 \end{matrix} \right\} \left\{ \begin{matrix} B_5B_6(B_7B_6)\# \\[1em] B_8B_9(B_{10}B_9)\# \end{matrix} \right. B_{11}: \quad \right|$$

13. *Degree of a node:* The number of edges which CONVERGE or DIVERGE (depart) from a node is called the degree of the node. The number of edges which diverge (depart) from a node is called the DEGREE OF DIVERGENCE of the node; and the number of edges which converge (meet together) in a node is called the DEGREE OF CONVERGENCE of the node.

Example 12: The Spanish sentence *Juan vino ayer*, analysed according to 'dependency grammar', can be represented by the following directed graph:

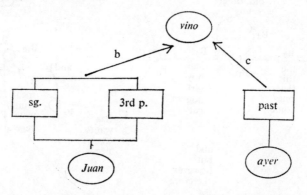

In this construction the verbal form is determined by means of the factors 'Singular (sg.)' and '3rd person (3rd p.)', inherent of the noun, and the factor 'past', inherent of the adverb of time *ayer*. The edges *b* and *c* converge on the node represented by *vino*. This node has a degree of convergence of 2.

Example 13: The Spanish noun phrase *el libro rojo*, analysed in the same way, would give a directed graph in which the two edges depart from the node represented by the noun, since the form of

both the article and the adjective depend upon the gender and
number of the noun. This node has a degree of divergence of 2:

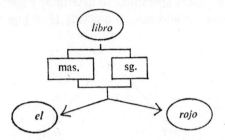

Example 14: The Spanish sentence *La madre compró un libro para
este niño ayer*, analysed in the same way, would give the following
graph, in which we have not specified the grammatical factors:

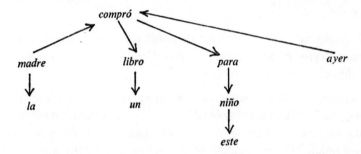

The node *compró* has a degree of 4: its degree of convergence is 2,
and its degree of divergence is also 2. The node *madre* has a degree
of 2, with a degree of divergence of 2; etc.

14. *Trees:* A CONNECTED GRAPH, that is to say, a graph in which
each pair of different nodes is joined by sides, that does not have
cycles, is a TREE. The graph is a TREE FROM A POINT if and only
if one of the nodes has a degree of convergence of *0*, and each one
of the other nodes a degree of convergence of *1*.

Example 15: The endings of adjectives which end in a vowel in
Spanish and the generation of the same can be represented by means

of a tree from a point: if we consider each node as a point where one must make an alternative decision (yes/no; +/—), we need a total of two logical operations to determine either of the forms. We would have the information quantity $H = \log_2 4 = 2$ bits:

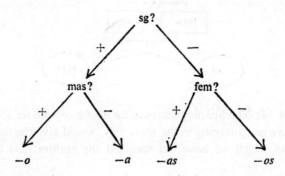

A connected graph is a TREE TO A POINT if within it only one node has a degree of divergence of *0*, and every one of the other nodes a degree of divergence of *1*.

Example 16: The process of generating the ending which corresponds to the Past Tense of the English verb, by means of selection and elimination of ambiguities can be represented in form of a tree to a point. The combination of the factors sg. and 3rd p. does not eliminate the ambiguity; the factor 'past' must be added:

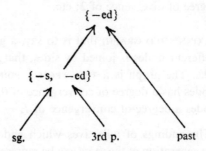

B. THE THEORY OF GRAPHS AND SET THEORY

1. *Definition:* A graph, sometimes called an ABSTRACT GRAPH, consists of a non-empty set V, of a possibly empty set E disjoint from V, and of a 'mapping' f of E into V & V. The elements of V are called vertices (or nodes), and those of E, edges. The expression V & V denotes the set of all the non-ordered pairs that are different and is called the unordered product of V with itself. f is called the 'incidence mapping', associated with the graph.

If $e \in E$ and v_1 and v_2 are the vertices so that $f(e) = (v_1$ & $v_2)$, it is said that the edge e is incident with each of the vertices v_1 and v_2, and vice versa. The following notation is also acceptable: $e \simeq (v_1$ & $v_2)$, which is read "e joins v_1 and v_2".

If V and E are finite sets — the empty set is included as a finite set — the graph G is called a FINITE GRAPH; should the contrary be the case, an INFINITE GRAPH.

2. *Directed graph:* Consists of a non-empty set V, of a set E disjoint from V, and of a mapping s of A into $V \times V$. The elements of V are called vertices, and those of A, arcs. The expression $V \times V$ denotes the set of all the ordered pairs of V and is called the CARTESIAN PRODUCT of the set V with itself. s is called the DIRECTED INCIDENCE MAPPING, associated with the graph. If a $\in A$ and $s(a) = (v_1, v_2)$, it is said that the arc a has v_1 as its INITIAL VERTEX, and v_2 as its FINAL VERTEX. The following notation is also acceptable: $a \simeq (v_1, v_2)$.

Given a directed graph $D = (V, A, s)$, its associated non-directed graph is the graph $G = (V, A, f)$, whose incidence mapping is defined: $f(a) = (v_1$ & $v_2)$ everytime that $s(a) = (v_1, v_2)$.

3. *Binary relations:* Directed graphs permit the definition of certain binary relations.

(a) A graph in which all the points of the relation are in a loop is called a REFLEXIVE GRAPH.

(b) A binary relation R is IRREFLEXIVE if in the given graph for each point of the relation v*R*v is not the case. In other words: the relation *R* is irreflexive if no point of *R* has a loop.

(c) A relation *R* is SYMMETRIC if $(v_1, v_2) \in R \rightarrow (v_2, v_1) \in R$. A symmetric graph is one in which for every arc a $\simeq$ (v_1, v_2) there is also an arc a' $\simeq$ (v_2, v_1).

Example 17: Every complete sentence conceived and felt as such should contain, explicitly or implicitly, a subject and a predicate (or a 'topic' and a 'comment'). The relation would be that "the topic needs a comment as complement and vice versa". The set *A* contains all the constituents that can fulfill the function of 'topic' and all the constituents which can fulfill the function of 'comment'. The relation refers to polarity:

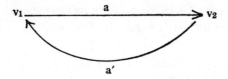

A COMPLETE SYMMETRIC GRAPH is a graph which represents a symmetric relation and which, also, is a complete graph.

Example 18: Combinations of the phonemes /a/, /r/, /t/ in Spanish:

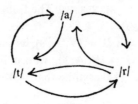

(d) A relation *R* is ASYMMETRIC if $(v_1, v_2) R \rightarrow - (v_2, v_1) \in R$. An asymmetric directed graph, for the same reason, is that in which there exists no side v_1, v_2 that has a corresponding side v_2, v_1. An asymmetric graph is complete when all the nodes are connected in an asymmetric form.

Example 19: The generation of the Spanish sentence *Juan está ocupado* in the flow of speech can be represented by means of a directed asymmetric graph:

$$\emptyset \longrightarrow \text{Juan} \longrightarrow \text{está} \longrightarrow \text{ocupado}$$

(e) A TRANSITIVE GRAPH is one in which the existence of arcs $a \simeq (v_1, v_2)$ and $b \simeq (v_2, v_3)$ implies the existence of an arc $c \simeq (v_1, v_3)$.

Example 20: Let us suppose that a machine may be in a finite number of internal states, and that on passing from one state to another it produces a certain symbol, e.g. a word in Spanish. The mechanism starts off in an initial state v_1 and ends in a final state v_4. Having advanced to the final state, the mechanism will have generated a sequence of words and eventually a sentence.

The sentences *The boy came* and *He came* have the same syntactic structure. In the following graph the nodes represent the states. Considering that both the constituents *The boy* and *He* satisfy the condition imposed by the verb *came* to integrate the whole structure, the graph contains a transitive relation:

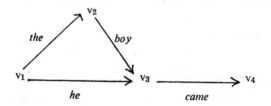

(f) A relation R is an IRREFLEXIVE COMPLETE ORDER if it is IRREFLEXIVE, ASYMMETRIC, TRANSITIVE and COMPLETE.

Example 21: Eliminating the edge v_3, v_4 of the graph of Ex. 20, a graph is obtained with a relation of a complete order.

(g) A relation R is of PARTIAL ORDER if it is IRREFLEXIVE, ASYMMETRIC and TRANSITIVE. It need not be complete.

Example 22: The graph of Ex. 20 represents a relation of partial order.

(h) A relation R is EQUIVALENT if it is REFLEXIVE, SYMMETRIC and TRANSITIVE.

Example 23: In the sentence *I hit it* the vowel in the word *hit* is short. If the vowel is lengthened, the meaning is changed: *I heat it*. Let us suppose that there are three individuals who are holding a conversation, on several occasions using the expression *I hit it* or another similar one in which appears the verb *hit*. So that there is no error in comprehension, the speakers should pronounce the vowel with almost the same length (condition of reflexive relation). Also, the length of the vowel pronounced by each speaker should be approximately equal to that of the vowels pronounced by the other two (symmetric relation). And finally, if speaker v_2 uses vowels of the same length as speaker v_1, and speaker v_3 vowels of the same length as speaker v_2 — the lengths, of course, are relative and not absolutely equal — than the length of their vowels should be the same as that of the vowels produced by v_1 (transitive relation). In the following graph the initial node v_1 represents the set of realisations of the phoneme /I/ by the speaker v_1, the node v_2 the set of realisations of the phoneme /I/ by speaker v_2, and the node v_3 the set of realisations of the phoneme /I/ by v_3:

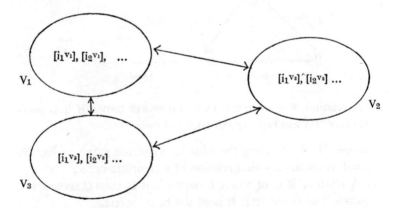

4. *Isomorphic graphs:* The graphs $G = (V, E)$ and $G' = (V, E)$ are ISOMORPHIC if there exists a correspondence as to V and E,

that is to say if they have the same number of nodes and if their nodes v_1, v_2 ... v_n and v_1', v_2' ... v_n' can be ordered in such a way that for any i and j the edge $v_i v_j$ is in the graph G if and only if the edge v_i' v_j' is in the graph G'.

Example 24: Analysing the following two Spanish sentences, in their constituents we obtain two isomorphic trees (connected graphs):

(1) *El regresó de Lima*   (2) *Juan compró tres libros*

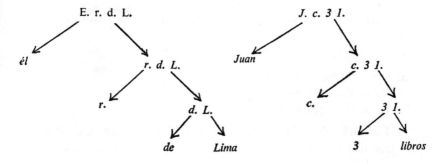

5. *Subgraph:* Given a graph $G = (V, E, f)$, the system $G_1 = (V_1, E_1, f_1)$ is called SUBGRAPH of G if and only if the following conditions are satisfied:

a. $V_1 \subset V$ & $E_1 \subset E$
b. $f_1(e) = f(e)$ for each $e \in F_1$
c. If $e \in E_1$ & $f(e) = (v_1$ & $v_2)$, then $v_1 \in V_1$ & $v_2 \in V_1$

Expressed in words: A subgraph G_1 of G consists of edges and vertices selected from G which have the same mapping as G, and with the condition that the selected vertices include all the end points of the selected edges.

Example 25: In the following graph, which represents the generation of the construction *John bought apples and went home*, the component v_2, v_3, v_4, v_2 represents a subgraph:

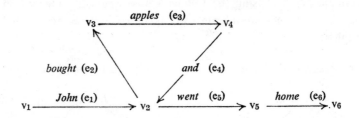

a. $V = \{v_1, v_2, v_3, v_4, v_5, v_6\}$
   $V_1 \subset V = \{v_2, v_3, v_4\}$
   $E_1 \subset E = \{e_2, e_3, e_4\}$

b. For each edge of the set E_1 of edges of the subgraph G_1 it is true that the same incidence mapping of E_1 into V_1 holds as in graph G.

c. If, for example, $e_2 \in E_1$, and $s(e_2) = (v_2 \ \& \ v_3)$, then $v_2 \in V_1$ and $v_3 \in V_1$.

6. *Edge progression:* EDGE PROGRESSION (or edge sequence) of length *n* is the name given to a finite sequence e_1, e_2 ... e_n of edges of a graph if there exists a sequence of n + 1 vertices (not necessarily different) v_1, v_2, ... v_n such that $e_i \simeq (v_{i-1} \ \& \ v_i)$ for i = 1, 2, ...n.

The progression is OPEN if $v_1 \neq v_n$, and closed if $v_1 = v_n$. If all the elements of the progression represent different edges, the progression is called CHAIN PROGRESSION when it is OPEN and CIRCUIT PROGRESSION when it is CLOSED. The set of the edges itself, without referring to the succession, is called CHAIN or CIRCUIT, according to the type of progression. This refers to non-directed graphs.

7. *Arc progression:* In a DIRECTED graph ARC PROGRESSION (or arc sequence) of length n is the name given to a sequence of arcs a_1, a_2, ..., a_n (necessarily not different) such that for a sequence of $n + 1$ vertices v_1, v_2, ... v_n it holds that $a_i \simeq (v_{i-1}, v_i)$ for $i = 1, 2 ..., n$. The progression is OPEN if $v_1 \neq v_n$, and CLOSED if $v_1 = v_n$.

An arc progression in which no arc is repeated is called a PATH PROGRESSION or CYCLE PROGRESSION, depending upon whether the progression is open or closed; the set of arcs itself is called PATH or CYCLE respectively. If the vertices v_1, v_2, ... ,v_n are all different, the progression is SIMPLE. A directed graph is said to be CYCLIC if it contains at least one cycle, and ACYCLIC if it contains NO CYCLE.

Example 26: The graph of Ex. 8 represents a simple path progression. The graph of Ex. 25 is a non-simple cyclic graph because it contains the cycle v_2, v_3, v_4, v_2 in which the vertex v_2 is repeated. The subgraph of Ex. 25 represents a simple cycle progression. The graph of Ex. 8 is acyclic.

8. *Connectivity:* A graph is connected if each pair of different vertices is joined at least by a CHAIN. Graphs which do not satisfy this condition are called DISCONNECTED.

A graph has a degree of connectivity k if each pair of different vertices v_i and v_j is joined at least by k chains which do not have common vertices, except for v_i and v_j.

A directed graph is STRONGLY CONNECTED, or simply, STRONG, if for each pair of different vertices v_i and v_j a path exists from v_i to v_j the same as a path from v_j to v_i, that is to say if the two vertices are reciprocally reachable.

Example 27: The following graph is strongly connected. It permits the generation of the following Spanish constructions, though not all of them are sentences. The edges represent the generative process of the respective element:

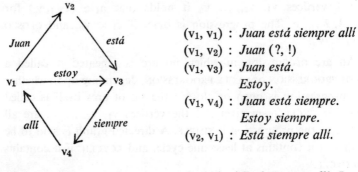

(v₁, v₁) : *Juan está siempre allí*
(v₁, v₂) : *Juan (?, !)*
(v₁, v₃) : *Juan está.*
          Estoy.
(v₁, v₄) : *Juan está siempre.*
          Estoy siempre.
(v₂, v₁) : *Está siempre allí.*

(v₂, v₃) : *Está*
(v₃, v₁) : *siempre allí.*
(v₃, v₃) : *Siempre allí Juan está.*
          Siempre allí estoy.
(v₄, v₁) : *allí.*
(v₄, v₃) : *Allí Juan está.*
          Allí estoy.

(v₂, v₂) :*Está siempre allí, Juan?*
(v₂, v₄) : *Está siempre.*
(v₃, v₂) : *siempre allí Juan.*
(v₃, v₄) : *Siempre.*
(v₄, v₂) : *allí Juan.*
(v₄, v₄) : *Allí Juan está siempre.*
          Allí estoy siempre.

A directed graph is UNILATERALLY CONNECTED or more simply, UNILATERAL, if in any pair of vertices, at least one vertex may be reached by the other.

Example 28: The following directed graph corresponds to the generation of the Spanish word *rata*. Not each pair of vertices satisfies the condition that both vertices be reciprocally reachable: the word does not contain the sequence /a/ — /r/:

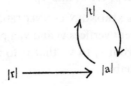

A directed graph is WEAKLY CONNECTED or more simply, WEAK, if in no pair of vertices are the two vertices reciprocally reachable.

Example 29: The condition is fulfilled in the graph which shows the relations of determination which exist in the Spanish sentence *Juan compró dos libros*:

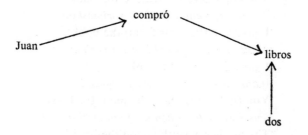

In this graph, the edge which extends from *Juan* to *compró* indicates that *Juan* (3rd person singular) determines the ending of the verb as regards person and number; the edge which extends from *compró* to *libros* indicates that *compró* determines the presence of a direct complement; and the edge which extends from *dos* to *libros* indicates that *dos* determines the plural form of *libros*.

A graph is DISCONNECTED if it is not even weak, that is to say, in such a graph there must be at least one vertex which does not join another vertex. A graph with only one vertex is called TRIVIAL.

9. *Geodesic:* In the theory of graphs GEODESIC is the name given to the shortest path between two vertices, and is denoted $d(v_i, v_j)$.

Example 30: The verb *give* has at least 4 different equivalents in Japanese, from which it is necessary to choose the proper one. Selection is determined by means of the following factors: grammatical person of the giver, grammatical person of the receiver, and social relation between the two. The equivalents are: *ageru, yaru, kureru, kudasaru*:

$ageru_1$:   *(Watashi wa)   anata ni hon wo agemashita*
            'I gave you (pol. form) the book'

$ageru_2$:   *(Watashi wa) sensei ni hon wo agemashita*
            'I gave the teacher the book'

ageru₃: Anata wa sensei ni hon wo agemashita
              'You (pol. form) gave the teacher the book'
ageru₄: Seito wa sensei ni hon wo agemashita
              'The pupil gave the teacher the book'
yaru₁: (Boku wa) kimi ni hon wo yarimashita
              'I gave you (familiar form) the book'
yaru₂: (Watashi wa) seito ni hon wo yarimashita
              'I gave the pupil the book'
yaru₃: Anata wa seito ni hon wo yarimashita
              'You (pol. form) gave the pupil the book'
yaru₄: Sensei wa seito ni hon wo yarimashita
              'The teacher gave the pupil the book'
kureru₁: Kimi wa boku ni hon wo kuremashita
              'You (familiar form) gave me the book'
kureru₂: Seito wa (watashi ni) hon wo kuremashita
              'The pupil gave me the book'
kudasaru₁: Anata wa (watashi ni) hon wo kudasaimashita
              'You (pol. form) gave me the book'
kudasaru₂: Sensei wa (watashi ni) hon wo kudasaimashita
              'The teacher gave me the book'

Vocabulary:

watashi	— I
wa	— particle of the subject
anata	— you (polite form)
ni	— particle of the indirect complement
hon	— book
wo	— particle of the direct complement
agemashita	— past form of the verb *ageru*
sensei	— teacher
boku	— I (familiar usage)
kimi	— you (familiar usage)
yarimashita	— past form of the verb yaru
seito	— pupil
kuremashita	— past form of the verb *kureru*
kudasaimashita	— past form of the verb *kudasaru*

Selection of the verb corresponding to each of the sentences given earlier can be made following the algorithms represented by means of the following directed graph, in which an alternative decision should be taken (symbolised by the signs — / + on the incident edges) on each vertex.

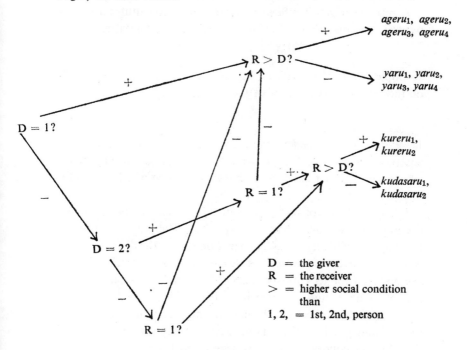

In this graph it can be appreciated, for example, that the vertex occupied by $ageru_{1-4}$ can be reached by various paths. The shortest path, departing from the vertex $D = 1$? is the one which passes through the vertex $R > D$? only. This path is the geodesic between the nodes $D = 1$? and $ageru_{1-4}$: $d(D = 1?, ageru_{1-4})$. Note, however, that the geodesic is the path which exists only for $ageru_{1-2}$.

10. *Reachability:* Reachability may be conceived as a relation within the set V of vertices of a directed graph. This relation is reflexive since each vertex of V is reachable by itself by a path of

length 0. It is transitive because if there is an arc progression A_1 from v_1 to v_3, and an arc progression A_2 from v_2 to v_3, then there is also a progression A_3 from v_1 to v_3. It need not be symmetric nor asymmetric, since, if there is an arc progression from v_i to v_j, there may or may not be a progression from v_j to v_i.

A relation which is reflexive and transitive constitutes a QUASI-ORDER; consequently reachability represents a QUASI-ORDER.

Example 31: In the graph of Ex. 29 the node *libros* is reachable on the basis of a relation of QUASI-ORDER.

11. *Partition and condensation:* By partition is meant the de-composition of a set S in non-empty subsets separated by pairs, whose union is the total of S, so that each element of S is in exactly one subset.

V may be the set of vertices of a directed graph G, and V may be decomposed into the subsets S_1, S_2, ... S_n. The CONDENSATION of the graph G with respect to this partition is then the directed graph whose vertices are these n subsets (each vertex being marked by the symbol used for its corresponding subset) and whose edges meet the following condition: there is an edge which departs from the vertex S_i to the vertex S_j in the new directed graph if and only if in the original graph G there is at least one edge from a point of S_i to S_j. The condensed graph is denoted by G'.

Example 32: The following graph, which represents the relations of dependence in the Spanish sentence *Nuestro profesor enseñó historia universal el año pasado,* can be condensed:

The set V of vertices of this graph may be decomposed into the following sets:

$$S_1 = \{v_1, v_2\}, \qquad S_2 = \{v_3\}, \qquad S_3 = \{v_4, v_5\},$$
$$S_4 = \{v_6, v_7, v_8\}$$

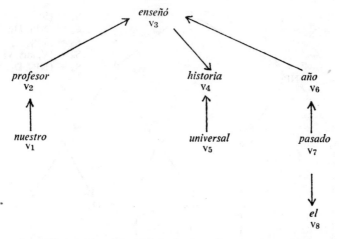

There is at least one edge which departs from a vertex (element) of S_1 to S_2 in the original graph G: an edge which extends from S_2 to S_3, and at least one which extends from S_4 to S_2 in the original graph; this means the conditions necessary for a condensation are met.

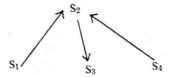

Example 33: Substitutions which are made in the following structure without destroying it are equivalent to a condensation. In this example the Spanish sentence *Mi amigo ha comprado un libro* has been analysed in its immediate constituents and then the constituents *Mi amigo, ha comprado* and *un libro* have been replaced by *él, compró*, and *libros* respectively:

Phrase-structure rules:

S	$\rightarrow$ NP$_1$ + VP		D	$\rightarrow$ *mi, un, el, ...*
VP	$\rightarrow$ V + NP$_2$		N	$\rightarrow$ *amigo, libro, ...*
NP$_{1,2}$	$\rightarrow$ D$_{1,2}$ + N$_{1,2}$		aux	$\rightarrow$ *he, has, ha, había, ...*
V	$\rightarrow$ aux + v		v	$\rightarrow$ *comprado, vendido, ...*

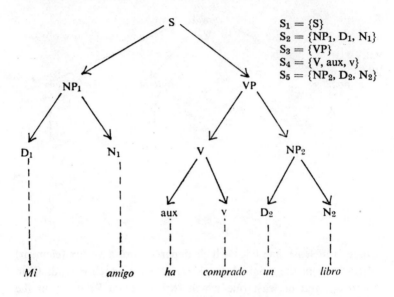

$S_1 = \{S\}$
$S_2 = \{NP_1, D_1, N_1\}$
$S_3 = \{VP\}$
$S_4 = \{V, aux, v\}$
$S_5 = \{NP_2, D_2, N_2\}$

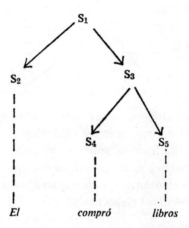

12. *Set of points reachable from a point:* The set R of points reachable from a point v_x is the collection of points V reachable from a given node v_x by means of a path, taking into account that v_x is reachable from itself.

Example 34: In the following graph, which reflects the relations of syntactic dependence of the Spanish sentence *Juan vendió libros ayer*, we have the following sets of points reachable from a point:

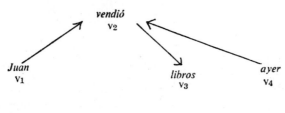

$$R(v_1) = \{v_1, v_2, v_3\}$$
$$R(v_2) = \{v_2, v_3\}$$
$$R(v_3) = \{v_3\}$$
$$R(v_4) = \{v_2, v_3, v_4\}$$

13. *Point basis of a directed graph:* The point basis of a directed graph is a minimal collection of points of the graph G from which all the points of the graph can be reached. A set B of points is a point basis of G if $R(B) = V$, the set of all the points of G, and if no proper subset belonging to B has this property.

A graph may have various bases. All the points of convergence 0 are in each base.

Example 35: In the graph of Ex. 34 we have the following base: $B_1 = \{v_1, v_4\}$

14. *Set of points which reach a given point:* This is the set Q of points $v_1, v_2, \ldots v_n$ of the graph, from which a given point v_i can be reached; it is also called ANTECEDENT SET $Q(v)$ of v.

Example 36: The following graph represents the concatenation of the English words *many, lots, more, of, the, people*. From the graph it is deduced that, if the preposition *of* is used, the use of the definite article is optional.

The set $Q(v_4) = \{v_1, v_2, v_3, v_4, v_5\}$:

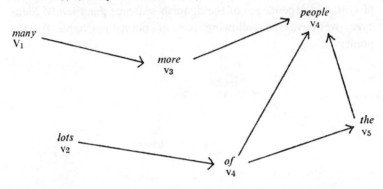

15. *Point contrabasis of a graph:* Point contrabasis of a directed graph is the name given to a minimal set S of points such that $Q(S)$ contains all the points of the graph G, or, in other words, $Q(S) = V$. Therefore, a contrabasis is a minimal set of points S so that each point of G may reach some point of S. All the points of divergence 0 are in each contrabasis.

Example 37: The following graph represents the concatenation of the English words *every, other, of, these, words, word* that is possible. Two expressions are obtained:

> *every other of these words,*   *every other word*

Node v_6 is reachable from v_1, v_2, v_3, v_4, v_6; node v_5 from v_1, v_2, v_5. Consequently $Q(S) = \{v_1, v_2, v_3, v_4, v_5, v_6\}$, which is the point contrabasis of the graph, since $Q(S)$ contains all the points of the graph G: $Q(S) = V$.

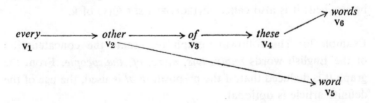

16. *Source of a directed graph:* When a directed graph has a base which consists of only one point, which means that all the points of the graph are reachable from that point, such a point is called a 'source': $R(v) = V$.

A directed graph may have only one source; in such a case it is called an ABSOLUTE SOURCE or a UNIQUE SOURCE. A directed graph has a source if and only if its condensation G^* has a unique source, or in other words, only one point with degree of convergence 0.

Example 38: In the graph corresponding to Ex. 37 the point v_1 is the absolute source since, from that node, all the other nodes in the graph may be reached.

17. *Negative source of a directed graph:* The node v_i of a directed graph is a NEGATIVE SOURCE, called a SINK if $Q(v_i) = V$. If the graph has only one sink, it is called ABSOLUTE or UNIQUE. A directed graph has a sink if and only if its condensation has a unique sink, that is to say, only one node with degree of divergence 0.

Example 39: In the graph of Ex. 36 the node v_4 is an absolute sink since that node can be reached from all nodes of the graph.

18. *The fundamental set:* For a node v_i, $R(v_i)$ is a FUNDAMENTAL SET if there is no node v_j in the directed graph G for which $R(v_i)$ is a proper subset. In this case node v_i is called the ORIGIN of the fundamental set $R(v_i)$.

Example 40: In the following graph the reachable set $R(v_3) = \{v_3, v_4, v_5\}$ is a subset of the reachable set $R(v_2) = \{v_1, v_2, v_3, v_4, v_5\}$. Considering that there is no reachable set larger than the latter, R(v₂) is the fundamental set of the graph. Node v₂ is the origin:

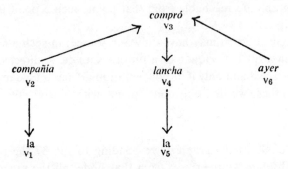

19. *The contrafundamental set:* CONTRAFUNDAMENTAL SET is the name given to a maximal antecedent set Q(v₁). In this case node v₁ is called TERMINUS.

Example 41: In the graph of Ex. 40 the set Q(v₅) = {v₂, v₃, v₄, v₅, v₆} is the contrafundamental set and v₅ is its terminus.

C. GRAPHS AND MATRICES

1. *General notions:* Directed graphs can be transformed into matrices. A matrix $f \times c$ is a rectangular order of $f \times c$ numbers called matrix entries, arranged in f rows and c columns. The entry on row i and column j of matrix M is denoted by m_{ij}.

2. *Adjacent matrix:* Given the directed graph D, its adjacent matrix $A(D)[a_{ij}]$, is a square matrix with a row and column for each node of the directed graph D, in which the input $a_{ij} = 1$ if the edge $v_i v_j$ is in D, and $a_{ij} = 0$ if $v_i v_j$ is not in D. The order of the matrix depends upon the order of the nodes, and upon the direction of the edges.

In an asymmetric graph a directed edge $v_i v_j$ implies that there cannot be an edge $v_j v_i$. In the corresponding adjacent matrix it is then seen that if the input $a_{ij} = 1$, the input $a_{ji} = 0$.

The totals of the rows and columns in the adjacent matrix show the number of edges which depart and end in each node of the graph. The total of each row of the matrix gives the degree of divergence and the total of each column gives the degree of convergence of the respective node. The total of the degrees of convergence of all the nodes of any directed graph is equal to the total of the degrees of divergence, and their common value is the number of edges of the graph:

$$\sum_{i=1}^{V} di(v_i) = \sum_{i=2}^{V} co(v_i)$$

Example 42: The following adjacent matrix corresponds to the graph in Ex. 20, which contains the ordered pairs (v_1, v_2), (v_2, v_3), (v_3, v_4), (v_1, v_3):

		v_1	v_2	v_3	v_4	totals of rows
	v_1	0	1	1	0	2
	v_2	0	0	1	0	1
A(D) =	v_3	0	0	0	1	1
	v_4	0	0	0	0	0
totals of columns		0	1	2	1	

It can be seen that in this matrix two edges depart from node v_1, and two edges end at node v_3.

3. *Incidence matrix:* The incidence matrix of the graph G is a matrix whose rows correspond to the vertices, and whose columns, to the edges, the entry being $a_{ij} = 1$ or 0, depending upon whether or not the jth edge is incident with the ith vertex. For a loop each entry on the column is 0. Considering that each edge is incident with exactly two vertices, each column of the matrix has two entries of value 1.

Example 43: The following graph represents the generation of the English expressions *a lot more apples, a few more apples, some more apples.* The edges represent the generation of the word in each phase, and the vertices represent the process from the beginning up to this point. In the incidence matrix the columns stand for the words which are generated in each phase, and the rows for the results in the context specified above.

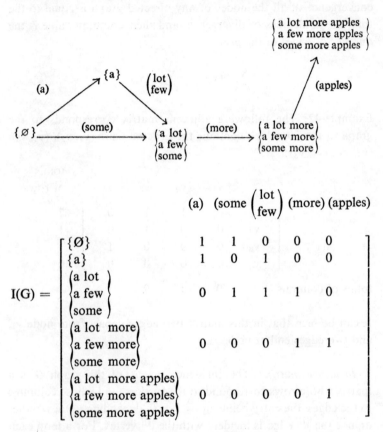

4. *Reachability matrix:* The entries r_{ij} of the reachability matrix $R(D)$ are defined as follows: $r_{ij} = 1$ if v_j is reachable from v_i; if it is not reachable, $r_{ij} = 0$. It is to be considered that each node is reachable by itself. The entries on the diagonal of the matrix are all 1.

Example 44: The so-called indefinite adjectives, articles, pos-
sessives and ordinals of the English language can be classified
according to the sequence in which they occur before a noun.
Thus *all*, for example, has to come before *my* as in *all my books*.
We establish six classes for this example:

$$A = \{a_1, a_2, ..., a_n \,|\, a_1 = \text{all, etc.}\}$$
$$B = \{b_1, b_2, ..., b_n \,|\, b_1 = \text{my, } b_2 = \text{the, etc.}\}$$
$$C = \{c_1, c_2, ..., c_n \,|\, c_1 = \text{first, etc.}\}$$
$$D = \{d_1, d_2, ..., d_n \,|\, d_1 = \text{several, etc.}\}$$
$$E = \{e_1, e_2, ..., e_n \,|\, e_1 = \text{other, etc.}\}$$
$$F = \{\ f_1, f_2, ..., \ f_n \,|\ f_1 = \text{such, etc.}\}$$

In the following directed graph, passing from one node to the next
in the sense of the oriented edges, admissible sequences are produced
in such a way that, at the beginning of the respective edge, the
element of the vertex is in front of the element of the vertex at the
end of the edge. In the graph it is also seen that there is no arc
between the vertices b_1 and b_2, which is interpreted in the sense
that these two elements cannot form a sequence.

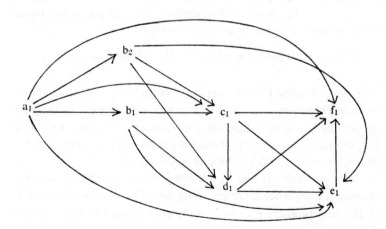

In the following matrix the vertices placed vertically represent the preceding elements, and the vertices placed horizontally represent the following:

$$
R(D) = \begin{array}{c c} & \begin{array}{c c c c c c c} a_1 & b_1 & b_2 & c_1 & d_1 & e_1 & f_1 \end{array} \\ \begin{array}{c} a_1 \\ b_1 \\ b_2 \\ c_1 \\ d_1 \\ e_1 \\ f_1 \end{array} & \left[\begin{array}{c c c c c c c} 1 & 1 & 1 & 1 & 1 & 1 & 1 \\ 0 & 1 & 0 & 1 & 1 & 1 & 1 \\ 0 & 0 & 1 & 1 & 1 & 1 & 1 \\ 0 & 0 & 0 & 1 & 1 & 1 & 1 \\ 0 & 0 & 0 & 0 & 1 & 1 & 1 \\ 0 & 0 & 0 & 0 & 0 & 1 & 1 \\ 0 & 0 & 0 & 0 & 0 & 0 & 1 \end{array} \right] \end{array}
$$

In the graph and in the reachability matrix it can be seen that the following constructions are admissible: *all the, all my, all the first, all the first several, all my first several other such*, etc.

On the other hand, the following are not admissible: **the all my, *the my several, *such several first*, etc.

The value 1 on the diagonal of the matrix does not signify that consecutive repetition of the same word is admissible, but it should be interpreted in the sense that any of these words may occur after an element Ø, i.e., it may be at the beginning of a sentence or phrase; or the element Ø may be one that does not belong to any of the classes established earlier, that is to say, it can be no word or one belonging to another class:

All books were sold yesterday.   He sold all books yesterday.

The entry of value 1 on the matrix only indicates the reachability without expressing whether it is through only one arc or through an arc progression. Thus, in the case of the entry $r_{a_1 d_1} = 1$ (all, several), the node d_1 is reachable from a_1 only through node b_1, through nodes b_1 and c_1, through nodes b_2 and c_1, or through c_1; but the two nodes a_1 and d_1 are not joined through only one arc because the sequence *all several* does not exist. On the other hand, in the case of entry $r_{a_1 e_1} = 1$, node e_1 is reachable through one arc but also through several, as is seen in the graph. Thus the sequence *all other* is admissible as is also the sequence *all my first other*.

5. *Distances matrix:* Let d_{ij} be the distance $d(v_i, v_j)$ from v_i to v_j; the distances matrix of the graph D, denoted $N(D)$ is the square matrix of order p whose entries are the distances d_{ij}. If there is no path from v_i to v_j, the distance $d_{ij} = \infty$, which means that $r_{ij} = 0$. On the diagonal of the matrix there are always values of 0 figure since the distance between each node and itself is 0. The entries represent the shortest distances. If all the entries of a distances matrix are finite, the graph is strong. Conversely, if it contains one or more infinite value, the graph is NOT strong.

Example 45: The following distances matrix corresponds to the graph of Ex. 44. Note that the entries represent the shortest distances between the two vertices of each pair. Consequently, this matrix does not, either, clearly reveal all the possibilities of combination. Thus, for the entry $d_{a_1 c_1}$, the value 1 is assigned because the two nodes are joined through only one arc, since the sequence *all first* is possible; but the same node can also be reached via node b_1 (or b_2), since it is possible to form sequences like *all my first* and *all the first*. In this case the distance would be *2*, which is not mentioned in the matrix:

	a_1	b_1	b_2	c_1	d_1	e_1	f_1
a_1	0	1	1	1	2	1	1
b_1	∞	0	∞	1	1	1	2
b_2	∞	∞	0	1	1	1	2
$N(D) = c_1$	∞	∞	∞	0	1	1	1
d_1	∞	∞	∞	∞	0	1	1
e_1	∞	∞	∞	∞	∞	0	1
f_1	∞	∞	∞	∞	∞	∞	0

D. MORE CONCEPTS WITH RESPECT TO GRAPHS

1. *Diameter of a graph:* The diameter of a graph is the term given to the greatest distance that exists in a graph between two nodes:

$$T = \max d(v_i, v_j)$$
$$v_i, v_j \in V$$

Example 46: The diameter of the graph in Ex. 44 is 4. In this graph various maximum distances can be found: $\max d(a_1, f_1) = 4$, the path which passes through b_1 and c_1; $\max d(b_1, f_1) = 4$, the path which passes through nodes d_1 and e_1; etc.

These maximum distances correspond to the longest sequences of lexical elements classified earlier.

2. *Associated number of pair of a point:* This is the ordered pair of the distance from a vertex v_i to a vertex v_j furthest from v_i, and of the distance from the vertex v_j to the vertex v_i. It should be remembered that we are dealing with distances which represent the shortest path. The first element of the ordered pair is the highest value in the row corresponding to the vertex in question in the distance matrix; and the second element is the highest value in the column corresponding to the respective vertex in the distance matrix.

Example 47: The index of the maximum distances from and to the nodes in the graph in Ex. 44 are: $a_1(2, \infty)$; $b_1(\infty, \infty)$; $b_2(\infty, \infty)$; $c_1(\infty, \infty)$; $d_1(\infty, \infty)$; $e_1(\infty, \infty)$ $f_1(\infty, 2)$.

3. *Radius of distances from and to a vertex:* The smallest finite number of the maximum distances in a directed graph — the distances being always the shortest path — is called the OUTRADIUS when they are 'from' a vertex. The smallest finite number of the maximum distances to a vertex in a directed graph is called the INRADIUS.

OUTCENTRAL POINT is the term given to the vertex with the smallest finite number of the maximum distances from a vertex;

and the set of such vertices is called the OUTCENTER. Analogically, the vertex with the smallest finite number of maximum distances to a vertex is called the INCENTRAL POINT, and the set of such vertices is called the INCENTER.

Example 48: In the graph of Ex. 44 the outradius $r_0 = 2$, which corresponds to the vertex a_1, from which it is possible to reach all the vertices within two steps. Linguistically, this should be interpreted to mean that the lexical element a_1 can precede all the other elements, whether directly or, at least, as a second element, as the case may be. This means, for example, that the sequences *all such*, *all my other*, *all my other such*, etc., are possible.

The same graph has as inradius $r_i = 2$, which corresponds to the vertex f_1, since from any other vertex f_1 may be reached in at least 2 steps. The outcentral point is a_1, which at the same time is the only element of the outcenter; the incentral point is f_1, which is the only element of the incenter.

4. *Networks:* When the edges in a directed graph represent some value — numerical or symbolic — this graph is called a NETWORK. A network may be more exactly defined as $DR = (V, A)$. A FLOW in DR is a function f of a numerical value defined in A. The value $f(a)$ is called the flow in arc a. If $a \simeq (_i, v_j)$, the flow goes from v_i to v_j as long as $f(a) \geqq 0$, and from v_j to v_i as long as $f(a) \leqq 0$.

The expression $v \rightarrow V$ symbolises the set of arcs in the network which have v as an initial vertex, and $V \rightarrow v$, the set of arcs which have v as a terminal vertex. The difference:

$$Q(v, f) = \underset{v \rightarrow V}{\Sigma}\ f(a) - \underset{V \rightarrow v}{\Sigma}\ f(a)$$

is called the NET OUTPUT at v, relative to f.

Example 49: Personal pronouns represent closed systems in every language. The positioning of a pronoun within such a system is possible on the basis of the elaboration of an adequate algorithm which, in optimal order, considers such factors as 'person', 'number', 'sex', 'object or human being', etc., and functions by means of alternative (yes/no) decisions, which can be symbolised by *1* (yes) and *0* (no). The transition from the pronoun nominal system of one language to that of another can be represented by a graph. In this example the graph shows the transition of the English pronoun system to the German, showing only the equivalents of the English *you* which are *du* for the singular, and *ihr* for the plural;[2] the selection of the German form requires the alternative selection — singular/plural. The graph shows a reversible process, that is to say, one can go from English to German and vice versa. On the basis of the alternatives the three pronouns can be coded binarily.

1st p: First person
2nd p: Second person
Sg. : Singular

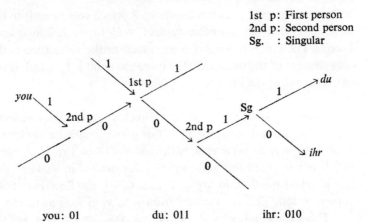

you: 01   du: 011   ihr: 010

This particular example, the coding of the English pronoun, represents a quantity of information $H_e = \log_2 2 = 1$ bit, and that of the German pronouns, $H_g = \log_2 3 = 1.585$ (since three alternatives are involved). If we imagine the process in the sense of first decoding the English and then encoding the German pronouns, that is to say, one is looking for the equivalents of the English pronoun, we shall have at node 1st p. an output of $H_g - H_e = 0.585$ bit, relative to f.

---

[2] Neglecting the polite form *Sie*.

Another way of calculating the output at node 1st p would be the following, making use of the binary system:

$$Q(\text{1st } p, f) = [(1 + 1 + 0) + (0 + 1 + 0)] - [1 + 0] = 100$$

5. *Abstract automata:* A CONCRETE AUTOMATON — for example, an automatic distributor of chocolates, cigarettes, etc. — functions in the following way: The device receives a CERTAIN INPUT SIGNAL — e.g. a coin of a certain value — and issues a CORRESPONDING OUTPUT SIGNAL, e.g. a bar of chocolate. The logical structure of a concrete automaton can be described mathematically. Such a description which represents a certain type of concrete automata, being so to say an abstraction, is called an ABSTRACT AUTOMATON, which can also serve to describe or simulate similar systems in diverse fields of science. Before formally defining an abstract automaton, certain conditions must be established.

(a) The input signals are DISCRETE, i.e. discontinuous: a time interval is required after each input signal and its corresponding output before a new signal can go in.

(b) The inputs and outputs should take place in a synchronised way, that is to say, that (1) all the inputs must themselves be synchronised, (2) all the outputs must themselves be synchronised, and (3) the inputs should be synchronised with the outputs. The inputs $x_1, x_2, \ldots x_m$ can be considered as elements belonging to the set X, called INPUT signals (or alphabet); and the outputs $y_1, y_2, \ldots y_n$ as elements of the set Y, called OUTPUT SIGNALS (or ALPHABET)

(c) The time intervals between the moments of production of the inputs and outputs should be CONSTANT and EQUAL, in order to thus facilitate a numeration of the moments of work of the automaton.

(d) The entry of the signals changes the internal state of the automaton at the respective moment. The set of INTERNAL states of the automaton is denoted by Z.

(e) The following internal state of the automaton, e.g. the state z_{t+1} at the moment $t + 1$ is determined by the input signal x_t

introduced at the moment t, and by the internal state z_t which already exists at this same moment. This can be interpreted mathematically in the sense that there is a function f which makes a new internal state $z^* = f(x, z)$ correspond to every input signal $x \in X$ and every internal state $z \in Z$ of the automaton: this function is also called FUNCTION OF TRANSITION. Consequently, the internal state z_{t+1} is defined by $z_{t+1} = f(x_t, z_t)$.

Finally there is a function g which assigns to each input signal $x \in X$ and to each internal state $z \in Z$ an output signal $y = g(x, z)$, which is called OUTPUT FUNCTION. The signal y_t which is emitted at the moment t is defined by $y_t = g(x_t, z_t)$.

On the basis of this explanation the following definition can be made: A quintuple $A = [X, Y, Z, f, g]$ is called an abstract automaton where f and g are a biunique mapping of X.Z into Z and X.Z into Y. An abstract automaton is called FINITE when the sets X, Y and Z are finite.

The abstract automaton can be represented by means of a directed graph. The vertices of the graph would represent the states of the automaton and the arcs, the possible transitions. From each vertex depart as many arcs as there are input signals $x_j \in X$.

Example 50: Let us suppose that an 'abstract' automaton receives words as input signals and that it conveniently processes these so as then to send them out in an ordered sequence in such a way that they form a sentence. The automaton could be denominated 'grammar'. In such a process the automaton would go from an initial state to a terminal state, once the sentence was produced; Such a grammar is also called a GRAMMAR OF FINITE STATE, for a sentence is a finite phenomenon. Let us suppose that the automaton receives the following input signals, not all of which change the internal state of the automaton:

At time t_1: x_{t_1} ... *Juan*

« t_2: $x_{t_2}^{(1)}$ ... *comprar*

« $x_{t_2}^{(2)}$ ... *sopa*

At time t_3: $x_{t_3}^{(1)}$ ... *dos*

« $x_{t_3}^{(2)}$ ... *est-*

« $x_{t_3}^{(3)}$ ... *niño*

« t_4: $x_{t_4}^{(1)}$ ... *libro*

« $x_{t_4}^{(2)}$ ... *saber*

« t_5: x_{t_5} ... *cantar*

The automaton should function in such a way that it reaches its
terminal state once a complete sentence has been produced. In the
following graph we have written the output signals inside rectangles.
It will be noticed that the output signals appear in the morpho-
logical form which corresponds to their value in the sentence,
excepting those signals which do not change the internal state
of the machine as they cannot be processed; they come out in the
same form as they had when they went in:

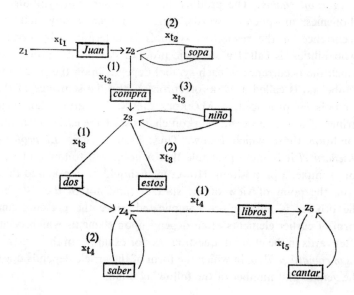

The automaton goes through the following states:

$$z_1 = \emptyset$$

$$z_2 = f(x_{t_1}, z_1) = Juan$$

$$z_3 = f(x_{t_2}^{(1)}, z_2) \ldots Juan\ compra$$

$$z_4' = f(x_{t_3}^{(1)}, z_3) \ldots Juan\ compra\ dos$$

$$z_4'' = f(x_{t_3}^{(2)}, z_3^3) \ldots Juan\ compra\ estos$$

$$z_5' = f(x_{t_4}^{(1)}, z_4') \ldots Juan\ compra\ dos\ libros$$

$$z_5'' = f(x_{t_4}^{(1)}, z_4'') = Juan\ compra\ estos\ libros$$

The output signal *(Juan, compra, dos, estos, dos, libros)* is defined by the output function. Thus, for example, the output signal y_2 *(compra)*, according to $y_t = g(x_t, z_t)$, is determined by the state z_2 (noun which in some way limits the selection of the element which may follow) and the input signal $x_{t_2}^{(1)}$: *comprar*.

6. *Markoff chains:* The production of a sequence of symbols — phonemes, morphemes, words, etc. — in such a way that the occurrence of the respective symbols is determined by certain probabilities, is called a stocastic process. A stocastic process in which the occurrence of each symbol depends upon the preceding symbol (s) is called a MARKOFF process, and the sequence of the symbols so produced, a MARKOFF CHAIN. In natural language strings of words represent Markoff chains since the earlier elements condition those which follow. Thus, after a chain *El profesor enseñará el* it is most probable that a noun will follow and not, for example, a preposition. However, it should be considered that, from the point of view of the speaker (and not of the listener) the process is much more complicated, since the presence and form of earlier elements often depend upon elements which occur afterwards in the chain in question, as, for example, in the sentence *Juan compró el libro*, in which the form of the article depends upon the gender and number of the following noun.

A MARKOFF GRAPH is constructed in the following way: The nodes represent the symbols (phonemes, morphemes, words, etc.) If a symbol A can be followed by another identical symbol, or, in other words, again by A, we draw a loop on A. To indicate that a symbol B can follow a symbol A, we draw an arc from A to B. And if A can also follow B, we draw an arc from B to A. If B occurs behind A with a PROBABILITY OF TRANSITION of p[A]B, the corresponding value is written beside the respective arc.[3]

Example 51: Let us suppose that we are interested in the degree of combinability of the three phonemes /a/, /b/, /c/ in a given language, and that the probabilities of transition $p_i(j)$ are as follows:

$p_a(a)$, that is to say /a/ can follow /a/: 0.0;
$p_a(b)$, that is to say /b/ can follow /a/: 0.8;
$p_a(c)$, that is to say /c/ can follow /a/: 0.2;
$p_b(a) = 0.5$; $p_b(b) = 0.5$; $p_b(c) = 0.0$;
$p_c(a) = 0.5$; $p_c(b) = 0.4$; $p_c(c) = 0.1$

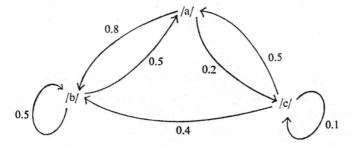

A Markoff chain can also be represented by a TRANSITION MATRIX. The following matrix corresponds to Example 51:

$p_i(j)$	/a/	/b/	/c/
/a/	0.0	0.8	0.2
/b/	0.5	0.5	0.0
/c/	0.5	0.4	0.1

[3] By probability of transition is understood a value between 0 and 1 which indicates the probability with which a symbol j can follow another symbol i.

Example 52: Let us suppose that one wishes to investigate the ease with which a student may distinguish the phonemes of the foreign language which he is studying. The corresponding test should contain the phonemic contrasts in the foreign language which do not have a phonemic function in the student's mother tongue. The phonemic oppositions (or phonemic contrasts) could be presented to the student verbally, and the student would have to decide whether or not there was opposition, marking an answer sheet.[4] Let us suppose that in 10 examples concerning a given opposition, the student correctly perceives the contrast in 8 examples, the input m_{ij} would be 0.8. In the corresponding matrix the values on the diagonal would represent the correct perception of the phonemes presented in the form of contrasts.

(student: perceiver)

	a_1	a_2	a_3	...	a_n
a_1	0.8	0.2	. .	...	. .
a_2	. .	0.6	. .	...	. .
a_3	. .	. .	0.9	...	. .
a_n	. .	. .	. .	...	0.4

(teacher: emitter) appears at the left margin adjacent to a_3.

A Markoff chain whose associated graph is strongly connected is called an ergodic Markoff chain. Therefore, it is one in which, given any state z_i, there is a probability $\neq 0$ of reaching any other state z_j, after a certain number of transitions.

Example 53: The production of the phonemes according to the graph in Ex. 2 represents an ergodic chain of the Markoff type if, considering that in an inventory of symbols (phonemes) not any sequence is possible, that is to say, no phoneme can follow any other phoneme.

[4]   See E. Zierer, "Test zur Untersuchung des Verständnis deutscher Sprachlaute für Spanischsprachige", *Deutschunterricht für Ausländer*, 16 (1966), 3-4 *Idem*, "La medición de la percepción de fonemas del idioma español por alumnos de habla japonesa", *Mathematical Linguistics* 25 (1963).

E. MORE EXAMPLES OF THE APPLICATION
OF THE THEORY OF GRAPHS IN LINGUISTICS

Example 54: We establish the following morphemic categories:

R_S ... root of noun
R_V ... root of verb
R_A ... root of adjective
R_P ... root of preposition
Av   ... adverb
p_V ... prefix which cannot occur on its own and which is placed
before the root of the verb
p_S ... *idem,* which is placed before the root of a noun
p_A ... *idem,* which is placed before the root of an adjective

d_{V-V} ... a derived suffix which is added to the root or stem of the
verb and which gives the complex the form of a verb
d_{V-S} ... *idem,* but it gives the complex the form of a noun.
d_{S-S} ... *idem,* that is added to the root or stem of a noun and
gives the complex the form of a noun.

The other symbols which represent derived suffixes are interpreted
in an analogous way.

The graph on page 50 illustrates the combinations which
correspond to the formation of the Spanish words 1-28 on the list
below.

(In this example the symbol R_S (root of a noun) has been considered
a form that corresponds to a noun with or without its original
ending. The same is the case for the symbol R_A (root of an
adjective), in which the suffix *-o* (or *-a*) is not considered a derivation
suffix. In the case of the noun *rearme* the suffix *-e* is considered as
a derivation suffix; this has been agreed upon *ad hoc* and does not
reflect any morphemic theory.)

The graph in this example has the following characteristics:
(a) It is incomplete, which means that not all the morphemes can
combine together.

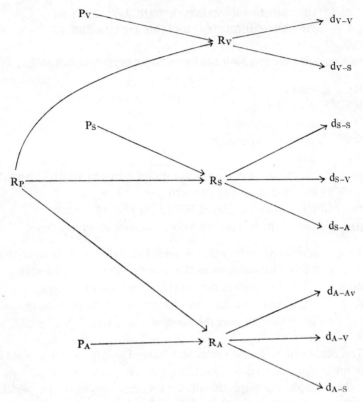

(b) It is a directed graph, which means that the morphemes cannot occur in any sequence; this restriction is also shown by the fact that the graph is weakly connected and asymmetric.

(c) The graph has a diameter of 2, which means it considers words formed by a maximum of 3 morphemes.

Example 55: The following graph represents a model of the process of understanding the English sentence *When he spoke, I listened*, when it is pronounced. While the listener is understanding word by word, he incurs 'expectations'. These expectations are fulfilled as soon as the words which follow are decoded, whether it be immediately or further on. The expectations can be ambiguous. Thus, after taking in the word *when*, the listener expects either a question or a subordinate sentence. Immediately he hears the word *he*, he discards the question and knows that he is going to hear a subordinate clause. At this point two new expectations arise in the listener's mind: That the subordinate clause (or dependent clause) will be followed by a main clause (or independent clause), and that the dependent clause, now begun, will be finished off, that is to say that the comment (predicate) will be added to the topic (subject). This expectation suggests a verbal phrase. Once the speaker has pronounced the dependent clause, the listener first expects the topic (subject), an expectation which is fulfilled as soon as he decodes the word *I*, i.e. a constituent that has a pronoun (as it could also contain a noun) as a nucleus. Then he expects the comment, that is to say, a verbal phrase.

In the graph, the symbols enclosed in rectangular boxes — nodes of the graph — represent expectations. The graph is a NETWORK. At certain vertices there is a confluence of information. From such a point information can continue only if information comes in from the opposite directions. This corresponds to the logical function of the conjunction: $1 \wedge 1 = 1$. On the other side, there are points in which there is a division in the information flow: Information can flow in one direction only if it also continues in the opposite direction. And finally, there is a point in which the logical function of the disjunction operates: The information continues either to the left or the right. The signal to eliminate the

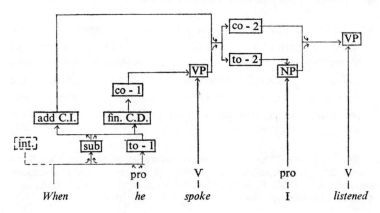

ambiguity stems from another source. In the graph there is a disjunction at the point from which a dotted line departs.

The arrows indicate that the graph is directed. From the psycholinguistic point of view it must be noted that the model is not complete, since it does not take into account such factors as intonation, social context, etc.

Key to symbols:

int:	... interrogative word
add C.I.:	... add an independent clause
sub:	... subordinating word
pro:	... personal pronoun
to-1:	... topic of the first clause
to-2:	... *idem* of the 2nd clause
fin. C.D.:	... finish off dependent clause
co-1:	... comment (on the topic) of the first clause;
co-2:	... *idem*, 2nd clause
V:	... verb
VP:	... verb phrase
NP:	... noun phrase

Example 56: According to the theory of A. Hoppe, language operates on the basis of a functional system, in which the functors and functions may be classified as follows:[5]

a. *Classification by level:* In every linguistic utterance two general levels co-operate: the level of linguistic contents and that of forms. When a verb requires a direct complement, the condition stems from the level of linguistic contents, being realised by the content of the verb in question. The fact that the Spanish preposition *entre* requires *yo* and *tu* instead of *mí* and *ti* —

---

[5] See: A. Hoppe, "Der sprachliche Formulierungsprozeß in den Funktions-ebenen der Sprache", *Beiträge zur Sprachkunde (Linguistik) und Informations-verarbeitung* 4 (1964). E. Zierer, "Las funciones en el lenguaje", *Lenguaje y Ciencias* 22 (December 1966).

contrasted with other Spanish prepositions — is a requirement at the form level.

(1) Functions between elements at the form level:

Example: The Spanish verb *aprender* requires that the infinitive which follows it be introduced by the preposition *a*.

(2) Functions between elements at the content level: In the Spanish expression *entre la mesa y silla* the preposition *entre* expresses the linguistic content of 'space' and 'two limiting points', which are represented in the expression by the words *mesa* and *silla*. Besides, this combination leads to a third, the one which requires the existence of something in the space thus defined.

b. *Classification by directions:* A function has a HORIZONTAL direction when it exists between two functors belonging to the SAME LEVEL; and it has a VERTICAL direction, when the functors belong to DIFFERENT LEVELS. Examples: '*aprender a* + inf.' (horizontal function); the function which departs from the element *entre* as a preposition to the content level, as was explained in subsection (a 2) is a vertical one.

c. *Classification by valence of functors:* From a functor can depart one function, several functions of the same type, and several functions of a different type. Also there can be functions whose dominant functor is necessarily a function of immediately inferior hierarchy:

(1) Monovalent functors: From a dominant functor only one function or several of the same type depart. Consequently, one has both UNI-MONOVALENT functors and PLURI-MONO-VALENT functors.

(2) Polivalent functors: These are functors from which functions of a DIFFERENT TYPE depart.

(3) Mediate functions: When a function has a function as a dominant functor, it becomes a MEDIATE function. Thus in the Spanish expression *entre la mesa y la silla* the functional relation that exists between 'space' and 'two limiting points' at the content level imposes the requirement that there be something in the space, or in other words, it plays the role

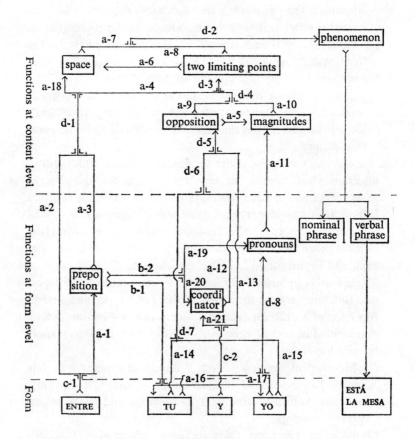

Fig. 1: Diagram which shows the interweaving of functions in the Spanish statement *Entre tú y yo está la mesa*.

a-1, a-2, etc. ... uni-monovalent functions
b-1, b-2,   ... pluri-monovalent functions
c-1, c-2,   ... polivalent functions
d-1, d-2, etc. ... mediate functions

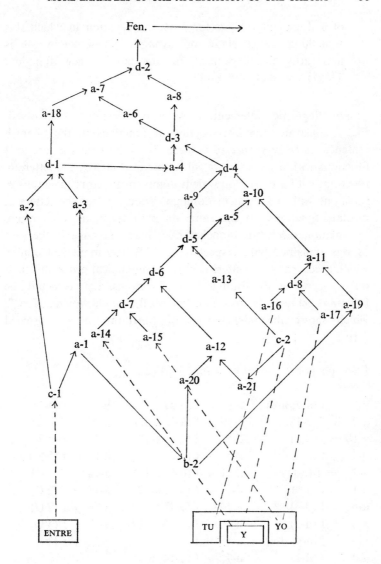

FIG. 2: Graph which shows the interweaving of functions. The arcs indicate the direction in which the functional relations exist.

of a dominant functor for a second function in which this something — a static or dynamic phenomenon — is necessarily the dependent functor in this new function. This is a mediate function.

In any linguistic statement, a series of functions is involved. Fig. 1 illustrates the interweaving of functions in the Spanish sentence *Entre tú y yo está la mesa*. In it the letters *a* represent functions with a uni-monovalent dominant functor; the letters *b*, functions with a pluri-monovalent dominant functor; the letters *c*, functions with a polivalent dominant functor; and the letters *d*, mediate functions. In the same diagram there are dots where information meets (or branches off); here the same is the case as was explained with respect to Ex. 55. The numerical indices which accompany the letters express no numerical order and their only purpose is to distinguish the functions. Let us detail the functions below, so as then to construct the graph shown as Fig. 2, which shows the interweaving of functions in a shortened form:

F (= phenomenon) = f (= function) (d-2)

d-2 = f (a-7, a-8)	a-9 = f (d-5)	b-2 = f (a-1)
a-7 = f (a-18, a-6)	a-10 = f (a-5, a-11)	a-20 = f (b-2)
a-18 = f (d-1)	d-5 = f (d-6, a-13)	a-21 = f (c-2)
d-1 = f (a-2, a-3)	a-5 = f (d-5)	c-1 = f (ENTRE)
a-2 = f (c-1)	a-11 = f (d-8, a-19)	a-14 = f (TU)
a-1 = f (c-1)	d-6 = f (d-7, a-12)	a-15 = f (YO)
a-6 = f (d-3)	a-13 = f (c-2)	a-16 = f (TU)
a-8 = f (d-3)	d-8 = f (a-16, a-17)	a-17 = f (YO)
d-3 = f (a-4, d-4)	a-19 = f (b-2)	c-2 = f (Y)
a-4 = f (d-1)	d-7 = f (a-14, a-15)	
d-4 = f (a-9, a-10)	a-12 = f (a-20, a-21)	

Example 58: The German sentence *Es wurde gestern getanzt* admits the following transformations:

(1) *Gestern wurde getanzt.*
(2) *Getanzt wurde gestern.*
(3) *(dass) gestern getanzt wurde.*

Let V be a set of 4 vertices each of which is to be occupied by one of the following words: *Es, wurde, gestern, getanzt*; A a set of arcs; and s, the directed incidence mapping of A into V × V such that a finite set of paths is produced that does not pass more than once through the same vertex, generating correct statements.

This graph will also produce the interrogative form:

(4) *Wurde gestern getanzt?*

		V_1	V_2	V_3	V_4	Sums
	V_1	0	1	0	0	1
A(D) =	V_2	0	0	1	1	2
	V_3	0	1	0	1	2
	V_4	0	1	0	0	1
	Sums	0	3	1	2	

In the graph and in its corresponding adjacency matrix it can be seen that the following sequences are not admitted:

> *Es getanzt wurde gestern*
> *Es gestern getanzt wurde*
> *Wurde es gestern getanzt*
> *Getanzt gestern wurde*
> etc.

In the adjacency matrix the entry $a_{v_4v_3} = 0$ indicates that there is no arc v_4v_3; hence, the sequence *getanzt gestern* is not admitted.

Example 59: The phrase *my small radio imported from Italy* does not cause any misunderstanding. However, if the same expression has to be translated into Spanish, certain decisions as to the inherent meaning of the English phrase have to be made. Thus the Spanish versions may be, for example:

mi radio pequeño, importado de Italia
mi pequeño radio, importado de Italia
mi pequeño radio que fue importado de Italia
etc.

Using set theory we can clarify the situation. We shall use the following symbols:

n   ... nominal nucleus: *radio*
a_1 ... attribute 1:   *my*
a_2 ... attribute 2:   *small*
a_3 ... attribute 3:   *imported from Italy*

Interpretation 1:   (a) There are radios imported from Italy.
                    (b) Among them there are also some small ones.
                    (c) Among these latter there is one which is mine.

In terms of set theory:

$$I(1): n \cap a_3 \cap a_2 \cap a_1$$

Interpretation 2:   (a) There are radios imported from Italy.
                    (b) Several of them are mine.
                    (c) Among the latter only one is small.

In terms of set theory:

$$I(2): n \cap a_3 \cap a_1 \subset a_2$$

Interpretation 3:   (a) There are small radios.
                    (b) Among them there are some which are mine.
                    (c) Among the latter there is one imported from Italy.

In terms of set theory:

$$I(3): n \cap a_2 \cap a_1 \subset a_3$$

Interpretation 4:   (a) Several radios are mine.
                    (b) Among them there are some small ones.

In terms of set theory:
                    (c) Among the latter there is one imported
                         from Italy.

$$I(4): n \cap a_1 \cap a_2 \subset a_3$$

Though I(3) and I(4) seem to express the same meaning, there is
nevertheless a difference. The meaning of I(3) is that ALL
my radios are small and among them only one comes from
Italy, and that is the one I am talking about. I(4), however,
implies that NOT all my radios are small. The equivalents in
Spanish would be:

   I(3): *mi pequeño radio que fue importado de Italia*
   I(4): *mi radio pequeño que fue importado de Italia*

Interpretation 5:   (a) There are radios which are mine.
                    (b) Among them there is only one that is
                         small.
                    (c) This same radio (the only one I have) was
                         imported from Italy.
In terms of set theory:

$$I(5): a_3 \supset n \cap a_1 \subset a_2$$

Spanish equivalent: *mi radio pequeño, el cual fue importado de
                    Italia*

Interpretation 6:   (a) There are radios that are mine.
                    (b) They are all imported from Italy.
                    (c) Among the latter, one is small.
In terms of set theory:

$$I(6) \; n \cap a_1 \subset a_3 \cap a_2$$

Spanish equivalent: *mi radio pequeño, importado de Italia*

Interpretation 7:   (a) There are several small things that are
                         mine.
                    (b) Among them there is one thing or several
                         things that are imported from Italy.
                    (c) That thing is a radio or among thoses
                         things is a radio.

Spanish equivalent: *mi pequeño radio, el cual fue importado de Italia*

The following graph can be considered a net in which we assign each arc a value $\cap$ (or $\supset$). The nodes represent n and its three attributes a_1, a_2, a_3. In this net the seven interpretations of the English expression can be found through 7 different paths, which must meet the following conditions: They must pass through all 4 different nodes, and may pass only once through the same node and the same arc.

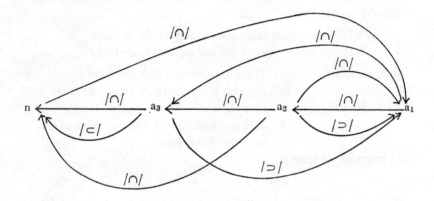

We simplify the graph in the following way:

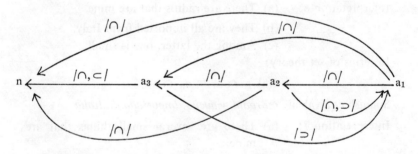

In the graph we observe that node n is a unique sink because it is reachable from all other points.

BIBLIOGRAPHY

Berge, C., *Théorie des graphes et ses applications* (Paris, Dunod, 1958).

Brodda, B., and H. Karlgren, "Relative Positions of Elements in Linguistic Strings", *Statistical Methods in Linguistics*, 3 (1964).

Busacker, R. G., and T. L. Saaty, *Finite Graphs and Networks: An Introduction with Applications* (New York, McGraw-Hill, 1965).

Cartwright, D., F. Haray, and R. Z. Norman, *Structural Models: An Introduction to the Theory of Directed Graphs* (New York, Wiley, 1965).

Chomsky, N., *Syntactic Structures* (The Hague, Mouton, 1957).

Flament, C., *Applications of Graph Theory to Group Structure* (Englewood Cliffs, N.J., Prentice-Hall, 1963).

Flechtner, H. J., *Grundbegriffe der Kybernetik* (Stuttgart, Wissenschaftliche Verlagsgesellschaft, 1966).

Ford, L. R. Jr., and D. R. Fulkerson, *Flows in Networks* (Princeton, N.J., Princeton University Press, 1962).

Gluschkow, W. M., *Theorie des abstrakten Automaten* (Berlin, Deutscher Verlag der Wissenschaften, 1963).

Hockett, C. F., *Language, Mathematics, and Linguistics* (The Hague, Mouton, 1967).

Kemeny, J. G., and J. L. Snell, *Finite Markov Chains* (New York, Van Nostrand, 1960).

——, *Mathematical Models in the Social Sciences* (New York, Ginn, 1962).

König, D., *Theorie der endlichen und unendlichen Graphen* (Leipzig, Akademische Verlagsgesellschaft, 1936).

Marcus, S., *Lingvistica matematica*, 2nd ed. (Bucarest, Editura Didactica si Pedagogica, 1966).

——, *Algebraic Linguistics; Analytical Models* (New York, Academic Press, 1967).

Meyer-Eppler, W., *Grundlagen und Anwendungen der Informationstheorie* (Berlin, Springer, 1959).

Ore, O., *Teoría y Aplicaciones de los Gráficos* (Cali-Comlombia, Editorial Norma, 1963).

Ortiz, A., and E. Zierer, *Set Theory and Linguistics* (The Hague, Mouton, 1968).

Rapoport, A., A. Rapoport, W. P. Livant, and J. Boyd, "A Study of Lexical Graphs", *Foundations of Language*, 2 (1966), 338-376.

Revzin, I. I., *Models of Language* (London, Methuen, 1966).
Schnelle, H., *Zeichensysteme zur wissenschaftlichen Darstellung* (Stuttgart-Bad Cannstatt, Friedrich Frommann, 1962).
Shannon, C., and W. Weaver, *The Mathematical Theory of Communication* (Urbana, University of Illinois Press, 1949).